THE ROMANCE OF HAPPY WORKERS

The Romance of ℋappy Workers

POETRY

Anne Boyer

COFFEE HOUSE PRESS
MINNEAPOLIS
2008

COFFEE HOUSE PRESS books are available to the trade through our primary distributor, Consortium Book Sales & Distribution, www.cbsd.com or (800) 283-3572. For personal orders, catalogs, or other information, write to info@coffeehousepress.org.

Coffee House Press is a nonprofit literary publishing house. Support from private foundations, corporate giving programs, government programs, and generous individuals helps make the publication of our books possible. We gratefully acknowledge their support in detail in the back of this book.

To you and our many readers around the world, we send our thanks for your continuing support.

LIBRARY OF CONGRESS CIP INFORMATION

Boyer, Anne, 1973–
The romance of happy workers : and other poems / Anne Boyer.
p. cm.
ISBN-13: 978-1-56689-214-8 (alk. paper)
ISBN-10: 1-56689-206-6
I. Title.
PS3602.O935R66 2008
811'.6—DC22

PRINTED IN THE UNITED STATES OF AMERICA

ACKNOWLEDGMENTS

Thanks to the editors of the following journals in which some of these poems first appeared: *Typo, Coconut, Diagram, Eratio, Denver Quarterly, The Poker, Wherever We Put Our Hats, Lit, Octopus, Copper Nickel, Shampoo, Fascicle,* and *Cannibal.*

"Always singing—Sunburn! Siberia!"

—MARINA TSVETAEVA

Contents

The Romance of Happy Workers

In the beginning we will begin
with Woody and his ideological kiss.

I can't put Siberia down
but can't keep holding onto it.

His lips were a proletarian meditation
on May, a battle between pathogens,

just those ordinary fears of newlyweds,
reformist or revolutionary. Saved

from drowning, I straddled
Woody on the Bolshevik mattress

and proposed like a furnace in August.
Not able to unite in a common struggle,

the marriage ended, a Trotsky and a mouse.

In the land of happy workers
the poets lived to harvest ice.

Hints of sparrow, rabbit, dogcall
mobilized the resident sundown

and the political lurch scurried
under verse reports of want.

One needed special bags for this
and a hyper-grade nocturnal habit.

I'm done gliding on the lake. Dedicated
to the class struggle, Woody serves

a dinner of quince paste and little else.
"Saffron Love" sounds Top Forty

in the country of chemical bliss.

Blatant as an industrialist,
these lies from the factory.

But how did art sound?
I'd say punchy, with action verbs

and the remote ratcheting of craft.
Offer alliteration on silver plate,

present two citrons, one flimflam soul.
The sublingual secret remained

grammatical but made no sense.
No one stole the heresy.

We never had such a thing as work.
All Siberia.

All the slick disappearance of what I loved.

I remember Woody's hammer, *par avian.*
He called it an experimental afternoon.

Once a week his manifesto flew
to my room. I'll admit nothing.

All the Czar's bassists, all the Czar's men:
Tyroleans mouthing Viennese rock songs.

These days Woody propagandas me under the sheets:
We are never better than the Workers!

There are no Workers left, I'd answer,
but his sickle is hard against my knee.

The Deus ex Machina Puppet Troupe
flew into Leningrad half past noon.

I waited among the Tartars bored
as moons. Woody showed, stinking

of pomegranate, gulag-eating grin.
I let him make a bed in my ear.

His rent cost nothing, two dummy rubles
and a half-spent roll of gossamer.

I babushkaed around his breath
100 mornings as if icons were Workers,

poems blocks of ice. My comrades say
leaving out meals will bring in the dead.

I would feed him what he wanted:
the cunning measures of production, stars.

Red giants slow dance, fire to fire,
burning up everything. This marriage

is a rumor we once heard.
The heroes of the People hum, like cicadas.

The People sound like us,
who never wanted to eat or sleep.

A Kremlin of lips. A Cyrillic vowel.
A Workers' harmony. A song might leak

out when silence is the acoustic remedy,
but how can we escape by foot an occupation of wings?

The year zero, I marked my calendar Dr. Zhivago.
I sing of love, a roulette tournament!

The morning of Woody's exile, I slept
for weeks. He accused me of waxing

aphoristic: *Happy Workers pledge themselves*
to the obstruction of their desire.

Workers who do not own the means
misprize it, find it hovers

overhead instead of sleep. Ophelia
barters for love, swallows silt.

Here rosemary. Here Hamlet's kiss.
Imagine at once a particle and its velocity.

Imagine your comrade's tributaries:
they all spill over for you.

A revolutionary has no principle
for uncertainty. Madame Tsvetaeva

reads his hand, feels Kill Creek:
this line here means your heart still beats.

Sometimes Woody eyes me
over his unhappy salad and speaks

of statistical probability.
We are like capitalists searching for paper clips.

Who could know that Cosmos 1953 would pass
under Cassiopeia in a memorable configuration?

How else might one catch a sustained glint?
The night was clear, my eyes maladapted.

I had never seen Mir so bright.
Written like parting, coupling becomes

a Pyrrhic victory.
Note Glasnost. Note Cosmonauts.

Note the gift thrown in the fire.

The Potemkin sailed on. Clichéd
as a martyr, Woody eats in my La-Z-Boy,

his heart on the leatherette pedestal.
We layered latitude over longitude

but never ended up anywhere.
Woody, why didn't you warn me revolution

would be so pale? The dining room
protests like elbows. The air protests like knees.

It's the music that degenerates.
I hold a compass to his left ear

and file papers for a waltz.
But how can one fuss

about our Hero of the People?
Gnat-size lapses?
Dinner? More tea-colored eggs?

1. This mercy I found in the end: when want was a Red Army,
   we were czars.

2. This mercy I found in the tunnels: in the dark I knew no light.

3. I am still looking for an exit without violence.

4. When we were young and could travel how I loved the look
   of the word *sortie*.

You Will Want Like Cowboys

I will want like splinters,
astonished spit, also like alphabets and minnows.

You will want at smallness,
also squirreling across the wire.

Wantings in the wilderness!
What did you think,

words?
You've seen it all before.

That's my last duchess—
all I want I've learned from her.

I want all I've learned from her.
Like Goya and church

you will fever like derangement.
You will lick no less

the ecstatic, and you will grow no more
accustomed to this dirty purse

than I to breathlessness
or pavement.

There is Kansas in the wilderness.
There is not cloudy.

All day the fingering, there your gaze,
there I will saddle up

the pillow, buckle, bobbin, tongue
I wanted from.

Sunsets Off

Nothing, too, is a subject:
dusk regulating the blankery.
Fill in the nightish sky with ardent,
fill in the metaphorical smell.

The horizon leaves the same
impression as runway: jet but air.
I wake to a grain bin, the end is near:
jimson and ditchweed, hog and trough.

The first beer can is making
high hopes out of everything.
No wheat is safe from chaff of this,
hullwrecked in Hugoton, thinking of sod.

Biplane

"raise high the roof beams"

Medusa hauled out her musclings
and stole a femur or some great leg or other.

None the ladder, she is a barn raised from contagion.

Then from the sky there storms the stormer,
plum-scared and Perseus. Watch that horizon,

for all heads fall there: all ruins: all breaks.

In a plain democracy blue skies are axes, axes are soap.
Perseus is a stuttering tendency. Medusa is a sod ear,

and the corral shudders with ponies: winged things.

Larks

Fourteen stanzas through the brush please mention
I dig this slumping anti-sentence: punctuation
a meter: yards up. Tight and unapologetic promoters
of the agenda—my ratty-down people—tell me
again how you grooved across my brother's face.
My concern is that you may flee rumbling en masse,
burning ship songs, the landing party on fire, stumbling drunk,
tongues flapping like surrender, hair in Albion curls.

Brave little sots, dandy in your bones (they fold like architecture),
do not hope for a minute I would not turret, moat, and knight for you.
I would Harvester and John Deere and Pioneer for you.
I would (if a creek) tadpole all the names I cunning
for you: preordain, prehensile, prepay, prescient, predate.
I cunning for you: mistake, misery, misalign. My people
(larks) I would catfish. I would bass boat. I would cast a fly.

Home on the Range

At the farm I slept on your heart.
That red organ throbbed.

Then the crop dusters dropped ticker tape.
The irrigation pipes waved.

*

Mix a drink of stock lot:
vermouth and the water table.

And the bar will smell of IBP.
And you will lick my Laura Ingalls.

*

Let's pretend our heartland's
green repair—

no John Deered plain,
just a pastoral *Moo*.

Hereford. Then thirteen
feet under the horny finger

of a bluestem root
we'll water witch—

all dazzling
and fortitude.

Provincial

Swearing from the silos!
Swearing from the inkjet!

Every starless city is
Every fat lip!

Swearing from the gurney!
Swearing from the Safeway!

Every paramedic is
Every cool kid!

Swearing from the Turin sheets!
Swearing from the folios!

Every word a funeral is &
the vowels fall

low with consonants.

A Reader for Those Who Do Not Live in Cities

—with all lines stolen from Carl Sandburg and Bertolt Brecht

1.

As nobody knew exactly what you wanted
let the crows go by hawking their caw and caw.
There may be some little thing not quite to your taste.

Look at songs
Hidden in eggs.

2.

We know you. It's no use your trying.

O farmerman.
Cram their insides till they waddle on short legs.
Kill your hogs with a knife slit under the ear.

What, still jabbering?

Hack them with cleavers.
Hang them with hooks in the hind legs.

Bring in what's left of him, we'll
Hold on to that.

3.
You were given a plate only.

4.

The walls are distempered after them.

Whoever leaves you only crimson poppies to talk with

they eat other bread.
Flinging follies of O-be-joyful
With the same sighs

*I am a hoodlum, you are a hoodlum, we and all of us are a world of
    hoodlums—*
Hanging from the same windows
maybe so.

5.

The woman I slept seven years with
Greets me politely on the landing
Smiling. *Let us be honest;*
the lady was not a harlot
until she married a corporation lawyer.

6.

The hieroglyphs of the rat footprints
chatter the pedigrees of the rats

It is practically an insult.

7.

It's important that you should hear me quite distinctly.
When you come back we may sit by five hollyhocks.
I have something to tell you which you will find of interest.

It is an idle and doctrinaire exploit.
You are a flathead.
If we were such and so, the same as these
Your respected mother has been saying so all along
Tumbling half over at the horse heads of the sun.
It's really exhausting.
Go on tumbling half over in the water mirrors.

(This record needs to be played more than once)

8.

Brancusi is a galoot; he understands birds and skulls so well.
He laughed and thought I did not mean it.
Is it only a dog's jaw or a horse's skull?
That shook him.

9.

I knew a hotel girl in Des Moines.
as if it were part of the arrangement.
The lightning bugs go a criss-cross carrying a zig-zag of fire
but try keeping snow in a saucepan.

10.

When I've been chatting with him
such a beautiful pail of fish.
He's speaking to me
anyhow it comes back in language just like that.

Cloven by Cloven

I have dined on the deviled, the pickled, the rude:
bacon, baloney, barbecue, maws,

neckbones, ears, feet, knees.
I sing the canned and the candied.

Hope farrows plate after plate:
origamied napkins, haikued tapas, all cast pearls.

The mediocre hope to sanctify the vulgar with prayer.
Psalms storm from fork to fork.

A steely pig won't be prayed for jowl by jowl.
A healthy pig will die of itself. Words won't Lazarus

       a sow
       rooting pokeweed,
       this self
       bristled, pink, compelled.

Ode O

I

Pocket Keats strokes our inners.

    Men sit and hear each other groan.

        Fiddle the crease where the page

Folds and unfolds. Fidget an O.

    Is love the haunt of flies? Dough,

        rising in the sultry, falling.

Flour scatters in monoprint.

II

etah I . Domestic. Damn it.

    The word rings a bell scratched

        Libertine. A cross-stitched apron:

Code for the self unsolved. The late

    Bird claims she isn't contextual.

        The universal soul sops until dawn, a wing

Bathing its feathers in Night Train.

III

Blame it on Fanny. She's been hot

    For verse, forcing her lips, letting the great

        Finger her fishnets. Per verse

He poured on her. Take my

    Airs, my overwrought breath, these lungs

        Consumptive with loathe.

O. O. O. The libertine bell.

IV

Darkling, who listens?
        Teeth, mewings, curlicues smashed
                Against pulp—who presses Romanticism on
Vellum? Who Os the Os? Each edition
        Wearies in its vowels and grows fainter
                Still. Typewriter. Linotype. Exact—
Breath against the firmament.

V

Nibs, nubs, India ink.
        Who sings of viewless wings opened?
                Who manhandles the daytime with sloppy
Quills? Woodcuts, etchings, candle
        Wicks, daisy chains, embroidery
                Needles darting in a hoop
Of moon. Moon. Hoop. Who?

VI

O who? O poesy
        Flowing over the cups of
                Monde. Let's admit it, habit has made us
Leviathan. Money, time, bawling
        Muses finagle chores, favors
                Come hither with eagle thighs.
(We open again for feathers.)

VII

A blackbird's foot fouls up
        The snow. Coo in unison the refrain
    .   etah I .etah I .etah I. Woo me a wormy

Iamb. Worry me, my

      Beakling. Imprint your wings against my.

           Awl. Thread. Bone glue. End

Papers. I'll stitch your seam. I'll bind.

VIII

This need facsimiled. The brain

      Perplexes and retards. I doodle

           A font of hate as long as the alphabet,

Embroider each towel with a fancy

      Work of hemlock. Xerox. Sampler,

           Simpler, plain little pain. Brayer hums

And prays (drink from this, the draught.

IX

Of fancy, the alien mimeograph. To think is to be.)

      To think is to be full of sorrow he lets loose

           In the after sweat. Keatsly, my indolent.

My sod pet. Stanza catfights with strophe.

      These are the odes of this week: Monday

           Loathes. Tuesday hates. Wednesday

Hits. The rest of the week, the same old.

X

O of ornery, inkjetting all over the page.

      Odious, the thought impressed. Yeast spins

           Itself crazy in our spitting and frothing.

Words are not dough. I hate everyone

      Who hasn't felt gingham bondage: my Lilliputian,

           The great his throbbing homunculus, the bird

Without alphabets frisking her toes.

Ode I

(Corrections in the Tenth Printing of the Twenty-Ninth Edition)

Strike I. A vowel with a posthumous existence.

Strike existence. If I turned into a feather I would give wings.

Erase feather. Replace with thorn. Give me the old poets and Robin
    Hood rugosas
hooking the jersey of the burglar's clothes.

I shall always imply. My sleep had been embroidered. My soul had
    become a lawn.

Insert: Pet-lamb, dieted with praise.

Strike gasp. My skirts had fallen. That faded, and I still wanted
    wings and to
scratch an itching that housewives should have their coppers scoured.

I am barely I. I grew up somewhere. I stayed home and planted
    Robin Hoods under
the south windows. They died before they snagged the thief who
    stole the I. I
died before I snagged the thief who stole the roses.

I ayes in the caucus of the soul. Roberts insists on decorum.

Strike decorum. The W A (or T, or knees slightly open). E, also
    A, and the
tempting wee E.

We speak in circles, the children giggling and/or fussing by our
    feet.

In referring to another member, he should, as much as possible,
    avoid using
his name, rather referring to him as "the member who spoke
    last."

I am the member who spooked last. I am not afraid to admit
    that I stutter
I, I, I.

>I<.

Remove >I<. A common tawdry. Who isn't oversaid. Who isn't a
    stud in the
lisping tongue or a twenty-pound barbell.

My closet holds a polyester corset, a velvet sans buttons, a paper
    sack of
overgrown clothes. I can't be i.

White out everything.

Disorderly words should be taken down by the member who
    objects to them and
then read to the member.

When the ink dries, can I fly away? I has mistaken herself for a
nightingale again.

Cowering under the wings of great poets rather than to a
    bitterness that I
am not appreciated, I enunciates with gusto, and as the great
    poet enunciated,
there is no greater folly than to enunciate gusto like a great poet.

Erase great. Erase poet. Erase no. Erase the I who confessed
    every sweat
that summer, even when we did that with only those, I and O.

Add emphasis to I contorting like O.

Insert I's aubade in the epilogue.

Ode Amo

"no animal can be a snob"—ALEXANDRE KOJEVE

I.

So I slip back into myself
Heyyo there old mutty, braying,

the clitoral nub of the cigarette butt
held like that, against two happy folds

or the exultation of monkeys brawling
shoulders all Linnaeus. My beast back

carries on in a courtyard of sparrows
with a shortage of poor Svevo who'd

make fumes of bird bones and valves.
When they do not fly: a plate displaying

appetite. It always grows. Smoke
in the company of some sterling fable

or smoke ringtails around morning—
or *Zeno, the implications!*—or I get you,

amore, odalisqued in the calendula
every ~~minute~~ cigarette, the last.

2.

Among the kohlrabi write everything wrong.
~~Amore Amo Amat.~~ What is paradise

but a red taverna and a brothel painted blue?
What about hair and fingernails?

If the intestines are resurrected, are they brim
full of shit? Physiology of the blessed!

If a thief lost a hand, but repented,
is it a stub or hand come back?

Say you pulled apart your sinews
and gave your flesh to all comers.

What will the end give you?
Beauty, who can again be a child?

3.

Tell a controlled fiction: Alex says
the sophist walks in crop circles,

never puts his/her prosthesis on.
He says, "Fuck you, be happy."

I wobble so spherically, an amputee.

4.

The story not so good had the reindeer
showed up and withered. ~~Mule.~~

In some afters we must steal our glittering
coup dé foudre's, burning little lexicons.

A traveler like Carmen, but less
of an archaeologist, Don José could clamor

thunderclaps. I'll storm no more of that!
Won't no longer so wander no coughing

so trembling at the sentiment braying I in I:
even John Locke claimed the Prince of Nassau's

parrot could talk sense, say "Homo Marinas."
and Paracelsus was such a fine scientist

putting his jism in the mare, cooing
this nature, all homunculi.

A Twilight of Minor Poets

(this is the cow with the crumpled horn)

1.

I once thought we were beautiful because we were beasts
I once found some pigs, so rumpy and pink!

Inconsequential! Sublimely compelled!
Dork pigs, quasi-canonically bent w/ grunt syllable.

2.

I once thought we were beautiful because we meant nothing

3.

I once thought we were beautiful because we were slant
or standing on our heels, staring out windows,
thinking some thing or other about light.

Or thinking on "some"—we were hesitant, humming,
stretched out—preludic—then

*Return we to Don Juan. He begun / To hear new words, and to
repeat them*

4.

I once thought we were beautiful because of "maraud"
"naught" "fuck" "fire" "morning" "fake"
"dismember" "decalogue" "cow"
"Ars" "Stars" "Hound" "How"

5.

I once thought we were beautiful because we couldn't make songs.
"Oh air, pride, plume, here—buckle!"

That White Rush

Were Fortune alone carnivorous.
Were its scarves the only tentacles.
Were it unzipped as we often are

as we are often only also fallen
empires and possibility, our thighs
slapped, opening at terrifying vague

fingerings—(yes, swan, yes)—
and were such screwings only the sure
screwings of Fortune, or were it only

Fortune after the screwing who
fidgets in the afterglow and moans.

(Fortune's song)

Of course you will see again my sparrows.
You will grow a thousand guileless corneas
On your fingertips. Even in the monster's

Beak or under the brute roofs of marriage,
Even in all jittering and aloneness and also
In your too muchness you will never fall again.

I will always be one of the marvels of your ocean.
I will always clutch at this dogwood limb
You lopped for me. And when the bleeding
Grows bored you will be master of your blood:

That tadpoles work against the wake—
that men or gods press their souls against bone
china and wash their forearms in sump—

that these rub their want into vernal ponds
or against the lips of a thousand women or gods—
that above a staggering species these beg

to mate against collapsing walls, also against
the light brawling black zeros, also against
dams and cities, also against the daily disemboweling—

also that my friend should shudder, be empty,
that his insides should upon me spill—
and that among these gutless fistfights and neckings
each still sets the other's broken bones.

What hearts but ours could drop
if we could fulfill all promise?

These that wait each night on the gangplank.
These that glow for us.
These that are elusive and witless as frogs.

GRIP

for Joseph Massey

Moon-sided, iconed, ill-considered
string of interludes   song:

a Russian girl with silver barrettes.

Oh silk along with everything.
Oh black of "hush" and "will."

The brunt of a sack: its asymmetry.

The brunt of the morning: a little gin.

People who think in lonely sentences are lonely.
Beasts who think in lonely sentences are beasts.

The cruel year,
the thimble,
the reconsidered weight,
the yearn.

Murk——————a dark mender.

To be thrown out on notice:

"There is so much——————"

or a word is a wire &
all along a small fire creeps.

+ A Little Poem for My Friends

You frogs listen.
The horizon knows what
It is saying here.

Lob

Stand fast. Grief is a gondola, a compulsive
label, a root canal—not a question of a single

switch at the center of things, but billions
of neurons, endorphins, titans rubbing
their wings. Let the monster wander. See a movie.

Buy new clothes. Clichés are bad manners.
Note this Hercules. I pull back, he claws

tighter. At best, it is an allegory
rather than an explanation. One stranger
keeps another company beneath

the leafy canopy. The heroine struggles
to fathom the questionable etiquette of grief.

I remember how it was to see David
on the tennis court. Fully explain that beauty—
the lingering molecules of scent,

the robotic insistence of daylight, then dark.

Domestic

Not the context for respirators. Not the ear
for severe exposure. Not the comb for adjacent areas.
Not the streetlamp for large rubber gloves.

Not bag your own. The checker should lay his furrow:
a tiff, a tangent, the red bananas, the sleeves made up with safety pins.
Surfaces should be worn. Lamps should smolder.

Dahlias do bloom like tumors. The birds do rise like bombs.
Context—a pink splinter: unfinished floor, bean leaf beetle,
hapless konza-vanicus. Certain volatiles.

Not the lie for that blue armchair.
There is a bed, but it won't go through the door.

Dinner for Two

We take the pyrex, eggs and creek
water, crawdads and starlings,

a batch of fins, wings. Slump
with a dinner from the fridge—

marinated America. Heat on one
burner, a red coil in a crowd

of Fire-king, depression ware.
If he pulls back his lips

to show his incisors, a song might
leak out. If he lets down the whisk

it might flatten itself into a diagram
of folded eights. The flesh might

breathe, the carrots go back to seed.

Fallible God the Square Opposite

Radish that way the moon addresses
the great adulterers: the slouching:

the black-seeded-simpson: the pitcher:

the jackrabbit: these admirers & silver that
way the water addresses the floundering:

the apostrophe: the white sigh: & the act.

As the mosquitoes shimmered mostly
a hundred luminescent in the falling day

got fat on my kneecaps (crave or I am

a complete wreck) on flight paths
the humans talk of bats & their particular

needs for houses caught in a clumsy

trot (the water) falls a hundred nights
falling addresses the falling dark

falls on my breasts radishes a fall

invented   the falls in this   address
incandescently as mosquitoes shimmer

privately as lit as falling as collides & slips.

Elegy

Across apocalypse thought con trails.
Across the dramatic monologue thought

          a wide wet tongue.

The calendula thought orange.
The fiction thought unduchess.

The cricketry thought
from the bray and the haw

of the mosquitoes stilled against
the skirmish. The end

thought the broccoli is left
to yellow the summer.

The human thought a blouse
waist and south thought Adam

thought of bass.

*

Flattery of animals
and their tongues and flattery
of silos and sentinels
and hospitals and were

*

The deer mouths don't like our beloved gray slabs.
Come out of your rectangle and look at me.

Nine ten up and down the elevation.
Come out of your rectangle and beloved me.

Snow peas, I don't like the great atmosphere sings.
Catfish, I don't like that I am thinking the blue

looks gone in this light and among the angles
there also the seascape and also among silos.

*

At the end me thoughter on flies
as tongues thinker
and flatter animals

and in this tonguer
the sows they thinker
they thoughter

*

One night thought on the jostling street.
That night imagined the jostling

in the alleyway, the singing of the feathered,
or the cats jostling on the lawn.

Or thought my smoke over the lawn.
Or thought the black ant who thought on my ashes

the black ant that considered ash food.

Sultanate

A tick, the back
of a thorax, one self

agape at cosmological
prongs. Aphids gaze

at a prelude, hunger
for lawn. Given

the hermeneutics
of pincers, one could

mouth a theory
of leafcutters, a feeler

in the fossilized
mumble. *Sure a mess,*

but a pattern shows
somewhere at a Delft

mill with wind
wheel, somehow in green

syntax after snow.

Bernoulli's Principle

Dork birds muck the cortical
                    folds: drunkening
that crows buck off gravity, the back lawn.

                    Not a day I don't want
to eat the beating of these wings
or eat the dirt turning on itself under wings, a spiral.

Oh Universe!

Twittering Atlas triggered
his handgun.

Dark turned street
lamp, on and off
as light

insists. The milksop
whined big

bang wasn't loaded.
Before water
cycle, horny nudges,
  Explosions seeds!
    Science love!

The suede impassive,
the good

lay, words grooving in
worn ruts,

  any less blasted—
   less splendid—
    less divine?

Poundcast

for K. Silem Mohammad

You let in the Song and the Song rotted your throat, and you yourselves out-songed the Song. Your allies in the victimized holdings are the strings. You stand for NOTHING but melody. And above metal melody, you have built a bank melody, and by that you WILL NOT be lyres. Corrupting the silence, you have lost yourselves to yourselves. And the BIG SONG has rotted EVERY ear it has wormed into.

An EARSTONE! Well, an exceptionally good swimmer MIGHT conceivably be cast into the sea with a song tied round her neck. She might perhaps unsing it. If she were a Lark, she would remember her jackfeather before being thrown overboard.

You seem to remember NOTHING. It was better you were infected with landscapes. As to the sea, there is no question of lyric in an ocean's proposition. It is as proposed a fleet of singers under Songry, as offered by planets and depressive ships and starling clouds of pirates and thieves.

Shakespeare and Bach are a velvet jacket. Architecture is a velvet jacket. Sculpture is all velvet jacket. Mr. Browning wanted a bright new velvet jacket, and art is (after all) only a prelude to piracy. One can conceive of a sighing in which there is NO economic velvet jacket. I mean absolutely NO VELVET JACKET for anyone.

It is much better, in fact, to conceive a fashion state than an art state: a state where in all arts are in wool and no art has much right whatsoever to velvet jackets—where even the pursuit— marvelous phrase that "pursuit of velvet jackets"—would be illegal, or at least regarded as a grave misdemeanor.

A really severe Puritan would probably tell you that the pursuit of velvet jackets is on a level with chippy-chasing. I know you don't THINK you are ripe for a real velvet jacket. You don't think YOU are ripe for the end of the fashion system altogether. You would rather such velvet jackets occurred in the Punjab or the sky.

For two centuries, ever since the brute billow brought 'em back into the Clouds, the soils have sucked out the billow's vitals. A mild penetration, for a hundred years they have bootlicked the billow's nobility and now where is that nobility? You had at least the semblance of atmosphere; you had, let us say, some air with the Lords of Diffusion as long as they WANTED the billow's titles, as long as soils WANTED to be addressed as Lord.

You could turn the worst edge of their ether, or rather you could turn it OFF the upper of huppar clawses and turn it ONTO the inner earth.

You could send 5000 airy pimps over to alphabets and give special flight suits, diplomatic, to inveigle the AIR into the billow's plans to get high fodder from Idaho and from Iowa, or to weld the billow's slave cellar onto the clouds.

The Relacion of Anne Boyer:

The True Account of the Journey during which she Discovers,
along with a Saint, that Liberation is Nothing

"I refrain from making a long story of it. Any one can
imagine what might be experienced in a land so strange."
—ÁLVAR NÚÑEZ CABEZA DE VACA

The first ministry of the body—a fundamentalism with metal.
Then the soul—the seasick whose bellies whimper.
Then heavings—caged.

This would sound better with a story in it!

The indeterminate night tendriling against metaphysics,
or the habitual mental position: a religious glow.

To the bucket, the screws and wing nuts of his/her kisses!
Liberation is not here. But where, Anne Boyer does not know.

"By setting on fire the scars of poverty, you will remedy the material," the Saint wrote, then burned. Cloistered in his abbey and blinking, he once constructed a wholly romantic mattress of imagism and a long wind. He puttered around gnawing at the heart's canonicals. And freedom, as freedom is fiefdom, was a liberation in prison's drag.

Continuing onward, we entered a firth.
Once I pass'd through a populous city.

> Anne, did you see liberation beside you, with silent lips, sad and tremulous?
> When it dawned the barges had been driven apart from each other, did you find a self in thirty fathoms and, drifting along at the hour of vespers, imprint your brain, for future use, with shows, architecture, customs, and traditions?

Anne, did love detain you for the love of you?
Anne Boyer rolled her eyes.

Cabeza de Vaca, where is your head?

Cabeza de Vaca, I love you!

I, Anne Boyer, who hate everything, love YOU!

Cabeza de Vaca, let's forget this convent and get the conquering on!

Cabeza de Vaca, who knows liberation is nothing, reminds me, Anne Boyer,

that I have ever wanted to be conquistadored. No tools, no iron, no smithery, no oakum, no pitch, no tackling. On every third day a horse should be killed. Liberation has lost forty men. During the tides of September's harvest moon, 1528, Anne Boyer thought on fingering the moss in Iowa and threatened love with a fistful of honeysuckle. Every day her thirst increases. The legs of her pony are worthless. She is wrenched and timid like Cortez.

> Cabeza de Vaca, I'm slipping!
> Cabeza de Vaca, Anne Boyer has read
> *Wretched of the Earth!*

> Cabeza de Vaca, I love you!
> Cabeza de Vaca, none of us escape art
> unhurt!

To this place we gave the name of Island of Ill-Fate.

On this island they wanted to make daredevils and witches of us,
wanted us to breathe on them and with that breath
they promised to drive the want away.

We laughed. They had to be kidding, but this was liberation—
we were breathing, ah down a neck, o in an eyelid, uh on a belly.

So on the Island of Poem rife with these pigs,
Anne Boyer, also, was breathing, and with all she could wreck,
breathing, and with all her breath telling all:

> *My sickness had prevented me. I was silence and disease,*
> *this religion, and also Anne Boyer, a woman in her thirty-*
> *first year, breathing hog breath, sow words, into sod ears!*

Can you now understand?
I was bound not to do anything and no longer slave!

Nearly four years I spent in the country, alone among them and
    naked, as they also were.

The Abbess of Exuberance is ever lewd. **Fingerfuckme!** she says to no one in particular, making a point of it, for politics. Confrere, there is only anaesthetic chastity. Let's have an orgy in the lexicon's motherhouse, everywhere screwing around and around. The humping, slick words: veritas licks vertigo, eros sucks off agape, and all these vocabularies are moaning, phonemes in heat.

Day by day and night by night we were together—all else has long been forgotten. The settler makes history and is conscious of making it. Anne Boyer is a skirt being hemmed. The first thing Anne Boyer learned was to pray in her place. This is why the dreams of Anne Boyer are always of muscularity. The wretched never conceive of liberation with open eyes.

There comes a time when the ending must end.

Liberation come-hithers, all pose—
   "Stay. Go. No. Never. I will eat you up. I love you so."

To know the first words beyond the old world—a lure.
Poem: a snake: once a tongue: in the ear church

all demon: all venom and capitulations: all havoc on cortical folds.

[In conclusion, The Reason for Remaining so Long]

At the end I got him to follow, hauled
his treasure across the inlets
and through four rivers since he could not swim.

Once I pass'd through a populous city
as if we are put on this world to forget our hurts.
Anne Boyer has read *Wretched of the Earth.*

I remained mine until the thirteenth
of the liberation, then leaked like a love note:
      Anne Boyer, I love you!

Thinking perhaps some snake had murdered me,
I returned to that regular cloister.
But how could this happen?

Good poets, she wept from her ears.

Valediction Forbidding Apocalypse

Dear tiny autumn of lizards,
dear pigs in attic marble,
dear pit / quarry / basement,
dear rock, dear stone, dear flesh:

remarkable this world
drowned anyway—a mass
transiently—this product
of the porous—or product of lions,

beaks, green shells. These sweeping
and consummate comrades—
this gun powder and this pasturage.
My Cid, where you might tremble.

"Sir Abbot!" cries Rudy Diaz
in the morning, the end aglow.

COLOPHON

The Romance of Happy Workers was designed at Coffee House Press, in the historic warehouse district of downtown Minneapolis. Fonts include Village and Viva.

FUNDER ACKNOWLEDGMENTS

Coffee House Press is an independent nonprofit literary publisher. Our books are made possible through the generous support of grants and gifts from many foundations, corporate giving programs, state and federal support, and through donations from individuals who believe in the transformational power of literature. Publication of this book was made possible, in part, through special project support from the National Endowment for the Arts and the Jerome Foundation. Coffee House Press receives general operating support from the Minnesota State Arts Board, through an appropriation by the Minnesota State Legislature and from the National Endowment for the Arts, and major general operating support from the McKnight Foundation, and from Target. Coffee House also receives support from: an anonymous donor; the Elmer and Eleanor Andersen Foundation; the Buuck Family Foundation; the Patrick and Aimee Butler Family Foundation; Stephen and Isabel Keating; Kathryn and Dean Koutsky; Mary McDermid; Tom Rosen; Stu Wilson and Melissa Barker; the Lenfesty Family Foundation; Rebecca Rand; the lawfirm of Schwegman, Lundberg, and Woessner P.A.; the James R. Thorpe Foundation; the Woessner Freeman Family Foundation; the Wood-Rill Foundation; and many other generous individual donors.

To you and our many readers across the country, we send our thanks for your continuing support.

Good books are brewing at coffeehousepress.org

Printed in the USA
CPSIA information can be obtained
at www.ICGtesting.com
JSHW080006150824
68134JS00021B/2306